TICKET TO THE
STANLEY CUP

MARTIN GITLIN

45TH PARALLEL PRESS

Published in the United States of America by Cherry Lake Publishing Group
Ann Arbor, Michigan
www.cherrylakepublishing.com

Reading Adviser: Beth Walker Gambro, MS Ed., Reading Consultant, Yorkville, IL.

Photo Credits: © AP Photo/Wilfredo Lee, cover; © KR image/Shutterstock, inside cover, 13, 19, 25, 29; © Nosyrevy/Shutterstock, 2, 3, 6, 10, 23, 32; © ZUMA Press Inc/Alamy Stock Photo, 5; © Gints Ivuskans/Shutterstock, 7; All-Pro Reels from District of Columbia, USA, CC BY-SA 2.0 via Wikimedia Commons, 9; Adamkgoodman, CC0, via Wikimedia Commons, 11; U.S. Army Photos by Eric Bartelt/USMA PAO, Public domain, via Wikimedia Commons, 12; Public Domain via Wikimedia Commons, 15; Detroit Free Press, Public Domain via Wikimedia Commons, 16; © Charles Mann/Shutterstock, 17; © AP Photo/LO/ASSOCIATED PRESS, 18; © AP Photo/John Locher/ASSOCIATED PRESS, 21; © AP Photo/John Locher/ASSOCIATED PRESS, 22; © Tribune Content Agency LLC / Alamy Stock Photo, 24; All-Pro Reels, CC BY-SA 2.0 via Wikimedia Commons, 27; © Darryl Dyck/The Canadian Press via AP/ASSOCIATED PRESS, 28

Copyright © 2026 by Cherry Lake Publishing Group

All rights reserved. No part of this book may be reproduced or utilized in any form or by any means without written permission from the publisher.

45th Parallel Press is an imprint of Cherry Lake Publishing Group.

Library of Congress Cataloging-in-Publication Data

Names: Gitlin, Marty author
Title: Ticket to the Stanley Cup / by Martin Gitlin.
Description: Ann Arbor, Michigan : 45th Parallel Press, 2025. | Series: The big game | Audience: Grades 7-9 | Summary: "Who has won the Stanley Cup? How did they make it happen? Filled with high-interest text written with struggling readers in mind, this series includes fun facts, intriguing stories, and captivating play-by-plays from one of hockey's most well-known tournaments"-- Provided by publisher.
Identifiers: LCCN 2025009137 | ISBN 9781668963890 hardcover | ISBN 9781668965214 paperback | ISBN 9781668966822 ebook | ISBN 9781668968437 pdf
Subjects: LCSH: Stanley Cup (Hockey)--History--Juvenile literature
Classification: LCC GV847.7 .G583 2025 | DDC 796.962/648--dc23
LC record available at https://lccn.loc.gov/2025009137
Cherry Lake Publishing Group would like to acknowledge the work of the Partnership for 21st Century Learning, a Network of Battelle for Kids. Please visit Battelle for Kids online for more information.

Printed in the United States of America

Note from publisher: Websites change regularly, and their future contents are outside of our control.
Supervise children when conducting any recommended online searches for extended learning opportunities.

Table of Contents

Introduction 4
History of the Game 8
Early Days, Big Moments 14
Modern Moments 20
Rising Stars 26

    ACTIVITY 30
    LEARN MORE 30
    GLOSSARY 31
    INDEX 32
    ABOUT THE AUTHOR 32

Introduction

National Hockey League (NHL) players all want one thing. That is to reach the Stanley Cup Finals. How do they get there?

It starts with the regular season. Teams try to win every game. They want to finish with a good record.

The NHL has 32 teams. They all play 82 games. Only winning teams make the **playoffs**. That is a series of games to determine the champion.

The playoffs are when it gets exciting. There are 3 rounds. Each round, a team must win the most games. There can be up to 7 games. The first team to win 4 games wins that round. The winner goes on to the next round.

The waiting is over and the big game is about to begin. Hockey fans, get ready!

These three rounds determine who will play in the **championship**. That is the event that decides the league winner. The two best teams go head to head.

Fans pack the arenas. Millions watch on TV. The winner is the NHL champion. They've won the Stanley Cup.

Let the big game begin!

The Stanley Cup trophy is famous. The current trophy was created in 1963.

History of the Game

Before the NHL, there was the NHA. That was the National Hockey Association. It began in 1909. It was only in Canada. Teams from Quebec and Ontario competed.

The NHA helped make hockey what it is. NHA games had 3 periods. They also had **penalties**. Penalties hurt a team. They are given when a player breaks the rules. They help the other team.

NHA team owners fought. They ended the NHA. All but one NHA owner met. They started a new league. It was the NHL. It started in Montreal. There were only Canadian teams at first.

Then the first American teams joined. The NHL had only 6 teams. It grew to 12 teams in 1967. More teams have been added ever since. Each team is from a big city.

Nick Suzuki is the captain of the Montreal Canadiens.

The Montreal Canadiens have won the most titles. That team has won 23 Stanley Cups. The Toronto Maple Leafs are next with 13. They are another Canadian NHL team.

The Stanley Cup is also a trophy. It was made in 1892. That was 25 years before the NHL was born. The Cup has gone to the NHL champion ever since.

The Stanley Cup weighs about 35 pounds (15.9 kilograms). It stands nearly 3 feet (1 meter) tall. It is presented to the winning team. It happens soon after the final game ends.

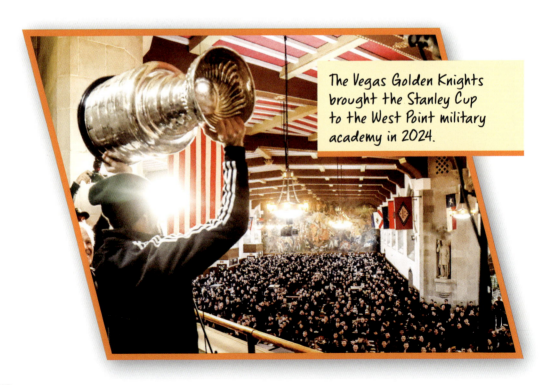

The Vegas Golden Knights brought the Stanley Cup to the West Point military academy in 2024.

The Florida Panthers won the Cup in 2024. They are one of 32 teams now in the NHL.

11

Signatures of the winning players are **engraved** on the trophy. That means the names are carved onto the trophy. Each player keeps it for one day. This does not happen in any other sport.

The Stanley Cup has been around the world. Players have taken it everywhere. It has traveled to Japan. The trophy has been in Switzerland. It has been on mountaintops. The Cup even visited an igloo in Canada!

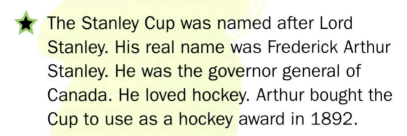

★ The Stanley Cup was named after Lord Stanley. His real name was Frederick Arthur Stanley. He was the governor general of Canada. He loved hockey. Arthur bought the Cup to use as a hockey award in 1892.

★ The Cup itself is a tradition. It is perhaps the most beloved trophy in sports. That is not only because players can spend time with it. It is because the Stanley Cup has been around for more than 130 years.

★ The Cup is older than the NHL. The league was born in Canada in 1917. The best hockey team in Canada first won the trophy over a century ago. And the tradition has continued ever since.

A BIT OF TRIVIA!

Early Days, Big Moments

It was April 10, 1934. The place was Chicago Stadium. The Detroit Red Wings were in town. They were playing the Chicago Blackhawks. The Stanley Cup was on the line.

The Blackhawks had already won twice. They needed one more victory. That would give them the NHL title. But Detroit was tough.

Neither team had scored. The game had to keep going. One **overtime** period was played. That is an extra period to break a tie. The score remained 0–0.

Then came the second overtime. The referee dropped the puck. It slid to Chicago player Harold "Mush" March. He smashed the puck with his stick. It slid past Detroit goaltender Wilf Cude. A goaltender protects the net.

Chicago Stadium in the 1930s before a Blackhawks game

March had scored the winning goal. The Blackhawks had won the Stanley Cup. And March was their hero.

He had also made history. His goal in a second overtime was a first. It had clinched the title.

Bill Cook almost did the same thing the year before. He played for the New York Rangers. Their opponent was Toronto. The Rangers needed one victory. The game was tied at 0–0. That forced an overtime period. Cook then scored a goal to win it. They did not need a second overtime.

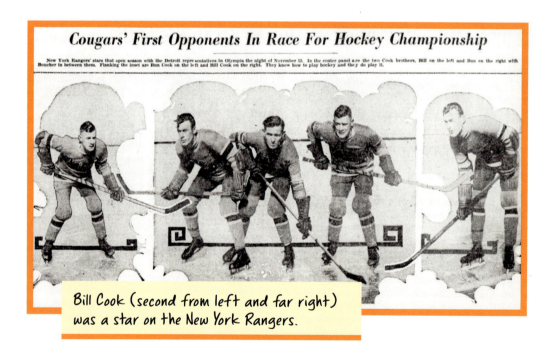

Bill Cook (second from left and far right) was a star on the New York Rangers.

And the crowd goes wild! Bill Cook had won the game for the Rangers.

The Montreal Canadiens were the best for many years. They won the Stanley Cup in 1957. That was 22 years after March's Chicago win. And Montreal kept winning. They won the next 3 NHL titles.

In 1960, the Canadiens made history. They reached the Cup finals again. This was five times in a row. Their opponent was the Toronto Maple Leafs. That was their biggest rival.

Toronto was no match for Jacques Plante. He was the Montreal goaltender. Plante allowed just 5 goals through in 4 games.

The Canadiens won Game 4 with a score of 4–0. That gave them their fifth straight title. No team has done that since.

Jacques Plante is pictured here in 1960 with Canadiens Coach Hector Blake.

Pete Babando was an average player. He played for the Detroit Red Wings. Babando scored just 6 goals in 1950. Most hockey fans didn't even know his name.

That made his Stanley Cup final effort amazing. Nobody expected it. Perhaps not even Babando.

It was Game 7. The Red Wings were playing the New York Rangers. The winner would take the Cup. It was a tie game.

The teams continued to battle. Neither team scored in the first overtime. The score remained tied. It was 3–3. So a second overtime was played. That is when Babando made the winning shot. Detroit won the championship.

WAY BACK WHEN

Modern Moments

Building a team takes time. New teams rarely win right away. But the Las Vegas Golden Knights surprised everyone. The Golden Knights won from the start. Their first season was 2017. They were not just winners that year. They reached the Stanley Cup finals.

The Golden Knights stayed hot. They posted winning records every year. Then it happened. It was 2023. Vegas was ready to battle the Florida Panthers. The Stanley Cup was on the line.

The Golden Knights won 3 of 4 games. They needed 1 more for the Cup. It was June 13. More than 19,000 people packed the arena. The fans were rooting for Vegas.

Jonathan Marchessault of the Las Vegas Golden Knights faces off with Florida Panthers goaltender Alex Lyon in the 2023 Stanley Cup Finals.

The team rushed in for a group hug right after the win!

Mark Stone was the Knights captain. Stone was a great player. He was at his best that night.

He scored in the first period. It was a **shorthanded** goal. This is a goal that happens when one team has fewer players on the ice than the other team. Short-handed goals are rare.

But Stone was not done. He scored again in the second period. That gave Vegas a 6–1 lead. The fans were in a frenzy. They knew what was happening. Their team was about to win. The Stanley Cup would soon be theirs.

Florida tried to come back. The Panthers scored twice. But Vegas was too good. Stone scored again in the third period. It was over. The Golden Knights were Stanley Cup champions.

A year later, Florida had another chance. It was June 7, 2024. It was Game 7. The Edmonton Oilers had won 3 games. So had the Florida Panthers. Both teams needed 1 more win for the championship.

Florida Panthers standout goalie Sergei Bobrovsky stopped shot after shot in a huge Game 7 victory.

The battle was tight. Both teams scored in the second period. One more goal could win it. Florida star Sam Reinhart controlled the puck. He skated down the ice. He bolted between 2 defenders. And he slid the puck past Stuart Skinner.

Panthers goalie Sergei Bobrovsky did the rest. He stopped every Edmonton shot. He finished with 23 saves. Bobrovsky and Reinhart were heroes. The Panthers had taken the NHL title.

The greatest hockey player ever? It might have been Wayne Gretzky.

Gretzky played for 5 teams in his career. He played for the Indianapolis Racers and the Edmonton Oilers. He played for the Los Angeles Kings and the St. Louis Blues. He also played for the New York Rangers.

He scored 894 goals in his career. He added 1,963 **assists**. Those are passes that lead to goals. That is 2,857 points. Nobody else has more than 1,921 points.

Gretzky led the Oilers to 4 Stanley Cup titles. He led the NHL in assists 13 years in a row. Gretzky won an amazing 9 Hart Trophies. He made 15 all-star teams. It is no wonder he was nicknamed "The Great One."

Rising Stars

Keep an eye on these rising stars. They might soon become legends!

Connor McDavid

The 2024 NHL season was soon to begin. Fans had a debate. Who was its best player? Many believed it was Connor McDavid.

That was amazing. McDavid was only 27 years old. But he was a superstar. He received the Hart Trophy in 2017. That is an award for the top NHL player. McDavid won it again in 2021. And in 2023.

McDavid did well in 2023. He scored 64 goals that year. That led the league. He added 89 assists. Those are great numbers!

Edmonton Oiler Connor McDavid took the NHL by storm.

Quinn Hughes and Jack Hughes

Meet Quinn and Jack Hughes. One plays great defense. The other is a big scorer. And they are brothers.

Quinn was born in 1999. He plays for Vancouver. Jack was born in 2001. He plays for New Jersey. They are both amazing hockey players.

Quinn won the Norris Trophy in 2024. That award is for the NHL's best defensive player. He also scored 92 **points**. Points are the combined number of goals and assists. Quinn scored 17 goals. He added 75 assists. His team made the playoffs.

Jack shined that year as well. He had 27 goals and 47 assists. He is considered a future superstar.

Quinn and Jack Hughes are brothers who play for different NHL teams.

It was the 1964 Stanley Cup final. The Toronto Maple Leafs trailed the series, 3–2. A Detroit Red Wings victory in Game 6 would mean a Toronto defeat.

The game was played in front of Detroit fans. That made it harder for the Leafs. They fell behind 2–1. Toronto scored to tie it at 2–2. Then the Leafs were losing 3–2. But they fought back. They scored another goal. They tied the game at 3–3.

Neither team scored in the third period. But Toronto Maple Leafs player Bobby Baun broke his leg. It seemed that he was done. Nobody thought he would return.

But Baun was not done. He refused to leave the game. He came back for the overtime period. Then he did something incredible. He scored the winning goal. Players often show courage. But Baun had given his team a title. And he did it with a broken leg.

AMAZING MOMENT

Activity

Study the NHL standings online. Learn what cities have teams. Then find out their logos. Figure out a way to learn all 32.

One way would be through a poster board. Draw a small picture of each team logo. One example might be a Maple Leaf. Another would be a Red Wing. Or a King.

Write the names on the back. Then study the pictures you drew. Try to remember them all. Invite a friend or family member to look at your work. Have them quiz you on the logos. See if you can get them all right.

Learn More

BOOKS

Herman, Gail. *What is the Stanley Cup?* New York, NY: Penguin Workshop, 2019.

Lanier, Wendy Hinote. *The Stanley Cup Final.* Mendota Heights, MN: Apex, 2023.

Streeter, Anthony. *Stanley Cup All-Time Greats.* Mendota Heights, MN: Press Box Books, 2025.

WEBSITES

Search these online sources with an adult.

National Hockey League Facts for Kids | Kiddle

Stanley Cup | Britannica Kids

Wayne Gretzky Story for Kids video | Bedtime History Stories

Glossary

assists (uh-SISTS) hockey passes that lead to goals

championship (CHAM-pee-uhn-ship) event that determines the winner in a league or sport

engraved (in-GRAYVD) cut or carved figures, letters, or designs into a material

overtime (OH-vuhr-tiym) extra period needed to break a tie game

penalties (PEN-uhl-teez) disadvantages given to a team that breaks a rule or advantages given to the other team in response

playoffs (PLAY-awfs) series of games played to determine a champion

points (POYNTS) in hockey, points are the combined number of goals and assists

shorthanded (short-HAN-duhd) in hockey, when one team has fewer players on the ice than the other due to a penalty

Index

A
activities, 30
American teams, 8, 10–11
Arthur, Frederick, 29
assists, 25–26, 28

B
Babando, Pete, 19
Baun, Bobby, 13
Bobrovsky, Sergei, 24

C
Canadian teams, 8–10, 18, 29
Chicago Blackhawks, 14–16, 18
Cook, Bill, 16–17

D
Detroit Red Wings, 13–16, 19

E
Edmonton Oilers, 23–27

F
Florida Panthers, 11, 20–21, 23–24

G
goal-scoring, 6–7, 13–17, 19, 23–26, 28
goaltenders, 6–7, 14, 18, 21, 24
Gretzky, Wayne, 25

H
Hart Trophy, 25–26
Hughes, Jack, 28
Hughes, Quinn, 28

L
logos, 30
Los Angeles Kings, 25
Lyon, Alex, 21

M
March, Harold "Mush," 14, 16, 18
Marchessault, Jonathan, 21
McDavid, Connor, 26–27
Montreal Canadiens, 8–10, 18

N
National Hockey Association, 8
National Hockey League, 4–6, 8, 10, 25–26, 28–30
New Jersey Devils, 28
New York Rangers, 16–17, 19, 25
Norris Trophy, 28

O
overtime wins, 14–17, 19

P
Plante, Jacques, 18
playoffs, 4, 10, 28

R
Reinhart, Sam, 24

S
Skinner, Stuart, 24
Stanley Cup Finals
  competition, 6–11, 30
  games and moments, 13–24
Stanley Cup trophy, 8, 11–12, 29
Stone, Mark, 23
Suzuki, Nick, 9

T
Toronto Maple Leafs, 10, 13, 16, 18

V
Vancouver Canucks, 28
Vegas Golden Knights, 12, 20–23

About the Author

Martin Gitlin is an educational book author based in Connecticut. He won more than 45 awards as a newspaper sportswriter from 1991 to 2002. Included was a first-place award from the Associated Press for his coverage of the 1995 World Series. He has had more than 200 books published since 2006. Most of them were written for students.